Be the News

A Guide to Going Viral With Your Human Interest Story

TABLE OF CONTENTS

BE THE NEWS

A GUIDE TO GOING VIRAL WITH YOUR HUMAN INTEREST STORY

To Craig, my beloved husband of 14 years and my partner for life. Your unparalleled support and kindness surpasses that of anyone I have or will ever know.

Preface

Despite having been a marketing strategist for 20+ years, I don't think I would have had the ability to write this book had I not personally experienced the landslide of attention one gets when the media decides you have something to say that they think people want to hear.

I don't mean to dis' the hundreds of press releases and media pitches I've written over the years, or even their media pickup success rate, it's just another story altogether when the media really grabs hold of a human interest story and doesn't let go.

My family's story became a national discussion when, after years of unsuccessful advocating for support for our mentally and organically disabled daughter, we made a decision to send her to live with another family in another state where she would be able to get the support that eluded us.

In part, this book is written from a standpoint of how the attention ensued, but more importantly, it's written from the standpoint of the mistakes I made having never been in the spotlight with a "commodity" story before.

I have used my personal experience rather than theory in Be the News. There are surprisingly few books written on this topic and I'm wondering if it's because so many rely on the media finding their story or on the theoretical ways to increase awareness by the old stand by's of advertising, promotion and press releases (See the Resources section to help you with these old stand by's).

While pieces of my story are woven throughout as examples of things to do and things *not* to do when you go wide with your story, it is not my intention to create an ego-centric venue. If you are interested in knowing more you will find a more comprehensive telling in the Epilogue.

My goal in writing this book is to guide you in your decision to go wide and fulfill your own mission of story telling. Whether it be to call attention to a social matter that most think is rare and isolated, or to tell a modern day fable with a good beats bad moral, if creating interest in your human interest story is your goal, you will find the in's and out's of doing so in the pages of this book.

The chapter's entitled *How to Steer Clear of the Tabloids*, *Who's Entitled to an Opinion*, and *Be Careful What You Wish For* are aptly named and are pages torn from the result of my family's story becoming a national discussion. Creating that national discussion is the best way to effect change. Being at the center of that discussion is not an easy place to sit, but well worth the outcome, for certain. Have I given you fair warning what this ride will be like?

I **am** very interested in YOUR STORY and hope to hear from many of you after you read Be the News. -----Lori Gertz

Chapter 1

What's Your Story?

*"There are eight million stories in the naked city.
This has been one of them."
The Naked City. 1948*

With the world's population at its highest levels and multi-tasking within that populace at exponential rates there are many, many, *many* stories to tell. What makes a story one of deep interest to others who themselves might feel duly owed coverage of their own adventure in life?

What makes your story worthy of front page news, being a guest on a talk show or being invited to speak on the Senate floor? It needs to incorporate a topic, though not one that has been played out, that is newsworthy in and of itself. A story whose underpinning is hinged on emotional conflict or one that has the potential for good winning over evil is nearly guaranteed of catching the interest of a journalist.

The retelling of an unimaginable, nearly impossible feat of human accomplishment is also the kind of fodder that most in the media hope to excavate. Journalists live and die by their next story. A story of one person taking on a behemoth issue or corporation is great, one admitting failure is even better, especially if it involves a child, a medical disability, provable dishonesty, the use of steroids in sports or a really great undercover opportunity. Stories like these will nearly always catch the attention of someone who's looking for the next great Watergate.

Of course, there's also the sad fact that journalists jump at any story involving a celebrity doing anything. Well, that celebrity example certainly puts things into perspective a bit. I've always found it especially disheartening that there are pockets of our human population that make the wires if they plug their own quarters into a parking meter or walk down the sidewalk in an atrocious outfit. It just doesn't seem right that there are really important issues not being covered in lieu of celebrity gossip.

But I'm not talking about that kind of questionably-even-news coverage here. I'm talking about the kind of stories that warm hearts and show (not tell) others that one can overcome obstacles no matter how great. I'm talking about stories that reporters and journalists salivate for because they stir an emotion, be it joy or rage, and that reporter's by-line becomes a household name as the story goes viral as first thousands and then millions are exposed to it by any of a bevy of social or mass media venues.

What is a human interest story?

Many news stories are focused on reporting the facts, especially those facts which involve money, sex, drugs or rock and roll. You might find this gets both boring and depressing after a while unless you have specific interest in the details.

While we might have a lot of interest in the election results, a cure for cancer, a food recall, or what tomorrow's temperature will be, news media may want to add local flavor or want to put a "face" on the news by covering a story or topic more in depth. This is sometimes referred to as the story-behind-the-story, the "better half" of a story, or the sidebar.

The human interest story may look at a news item in a more personal, emotional way. This is accomplished by pressing the flesh with people who have been directly affected by it or creating a report on one or several people facing challenges that it may have uncovered. The mission of covering these stories is to grab us by our emotional shirt collars and make us think and form an opinion.

It's rare to see a nightly newscast or a morning newspaper without at least one human interest story. Most have a standard location for them, in broadcast, it is often the last story told before signoff.

A newspaper might be covering post-hurricane financial losses and have an article that deals with statistics regarding them. To push past the grind, they might have a sidebar article on a few people in the town that is rebuilding. The main topic is the hurricane, but the underlying emotional piece is how it affected people, like you and me. It gives a whole new paradigm to understanding the losses and puts them in a feeling perspective – beyond the facts.

In contrast to a regular and objective news story, the rules of journalism are bit looser, dare

I say, even slightly more subjective with human interest topics. In some cases the story is so intense that the reporter barely needs more than the facts as they are reported. Other times, the story needs to be reigned in. A slant is sometimes created and then the job of the human interest story is to add perspective rather than the opposite happening.

If yours is a human interest story, it doesn't have to be deeply stirring and emotional, just on-topic or perhaps more for light laughs (if that falls within your goal for going wide with it to begin with). This is especially true when news venues are leading with gory, crime laden flavored journalism. Stories that meet neither of those end goals can make it into the news just as a diversion to the hard stuff to make it more palatable to the viewer. If the lighter material wasn't there, readers and viewers would sooner turn the page or the channel to avoid the ugly news.

What makes your story newsworthy?

Is your story one of Davy and Goliath? There are archetype stories, no doubt, that if you follow a set content structure you can recreate and garner interest. Everyone loves a story of the small guy coming out on top. But they also love AND hate and don't forget *loving to hate* stories of failure and humiliation as much as they like reading about random acts of kindness.

Just like the target audiences for different movie genres, there are target audiences for different story genres. Association is key. Can the target audience relate to you or what happened to you? It has to be believable, even if they choose not to believe your retelling of it.

So what is your story? And more importantly, for you to have skin in the game, which you surely will when your story gets picked up, what is your mission in telling it? This is different than your positioning statement. This is where is gets personal for you. The subtlety here is that it's personal but not centered on you.

If your mission is you-centric, stop before you start. If you are not a celebrity in your own right, few journalists or reporters are going to make you one, no matter how bizarre your story is. And if you do, by chance, get someone to pick up a story that is completely ego-driven, watch out for the commentary that will follow.

I cover that more in the chapter entitled *Who's Entitled to an Opinion.*

On the contrary, if your mission is to tell your story to help others whether it is by increasing awareness of an ongoing issue or topic that is going unfunded or unattended to, or through launching a new initiative that will work towards a more sustainable future for our planet, then you are on the right track. Even though the most credible five-star journalists have their eyes and ears open for stories that work towards a greater good or uncover some unjust practice, their ears really perk up when there is an element of some erstwhile do-no-good'er who can be called out on the rug for a public lashing.

What do you hope to accomplish by telling your story?

Before pitching your story to the media, write a personal mission statement for yourself highlighting what you hope to accomplish by going wide with your story. Find your inner truth, no matter how much digging you must do, because if you don't, the judgers and haters will create one for you and it won't resemble, in the least, the one you might have created for yourself.

Is your mission to effect change in social or public policy? Is it to call attention to injustice or unfairness in something that affects a large group of people? Is it to raise awareness for a significantly smaller population whose disability prohibits them from getting vocal themselves? Can and will your story create enough debate and interest to perhaps shift the weight on legislature on a local, state or federal basis? Aim high with your mission. I believe that setting the intention for great rewards will result in a greater realization of those dreams.

If you have your eye on the goal and the reason you are willing to open your life up like a book for others to read in the first place, it will save you much grief and give you a stronger foundation on which to stand after the media hype calms down. Don't forget, while your story might be a flash in the pan on a national or even international level, you still have to look at yourself in the mirror and know you told your truth for the rest of your life.

Do your research!

Research sounds like something you would otherwise rely on the journalist taking your story to handle, but it's the lynchpin of getting someone to listen to you to begin with.

When you prove that you faced down a behemoth that has affected thousands or hundreds of thousands of others, your story becomes a 'representative' story. It's no longer just about you; it's about a LOT of people. You go from being one person to representing a whole segment of the public that is in some way affected by an issue.

If you are willing to talk about something that others push under the rug out of embarrassment or fear of humiliation, you will become the "spokesperson" for the others and will soon find yourself part of a club of incredibly supportive members. This may come as your biggest surprise when you may have thought that no one could even imagine the story you lived, no less have had one just like it.

Like the old saying, all that is old is new again; one's story is never the first time it has been lived. However, many stories are never told, or at least not until you are ready to represent the group of those that lived it before you.

Find supportive research from credible sources to tie into your story by tapping government resources like the census or the Department of Health and Human Services. Utilize national organizations that are related to the issue or the experience you faced. Tying a national organization's supportive research or getting a quote of support from someone who regularly provides sound bites to the media is an excellent way to establish quick and easy credibility. It almost immediately validates the need for the retelling of your story when a national organization or action committee has devoted resources to the issue at hand.

One great source for identifying organizations, associations and societies is the Encyclopedia of Associations, published by Gale Research Company. It features 23,000 national and international organizations and is available in most public libraries. If you want to access online, you can find it on infoplease.com.

Wikipedia sports a pretty comprehensive list of industry trade groups and places like the U.S. Department of Education offer extensive lists in its Education Resource and Organizations directory. (See the Resources page in the back for more specifics).

Another method to getting attention from a journalist is your public position as a local spokesperson/advocate for a national organization, even if it's on a local level you will benefit from aligning with an organization that has only the public's interest at heart.

Piggyback your story on a national news item

Read, read, and read some more. Blogs. Books. Newspapers. Magazines. I envision your desks littered with clippings and collections of excel sheets lined with links to stories and topics related to your story-line.

Many news-related sites, weblogs and other online publishers syndicate their content as an **RSS Feed** to whoever wants it. Identify some keywords that come up in the issues surrounding your topic and use those keywords to find news sites that offer relevant news. Google, Yahoo and just about every search engine offers a keyword and wordtracker tool. Consider using a sequence or phrase of words to track more specific research. For example, you could track the keywords "mental illness", or you could get more specific and track the phrase, "mental illness and violence"

Through Google alerts, you can identify keywords that are important to you and whenever Google finds them in their seo scouring, they will email you a link with a preview of the article they appeared in. I have used Google alerts for years as the easiest tool to watch for where my name and the term FASD is being used. It also puts me at the forefront of getting the news on those terms, sometimes before anyone else. This really helps my credibility as a source of information and support on my facebook, twitter and other social media feeds where I then post the articles I have been alerted to.

Subscribe to **RSS Feeds** and Google alerts to keywords related to the content of your story and feel confident you will be scouring the internet for on-point articles and discussions that give your story more weight and you more credibility.

When you locate a newsworthy topic that relates to your story and can piggyback it onto a national issue, you will find much more interest and responsiveness from the media.

There's endless space on the internet and countless journalists, writers, bloggers, and reporters have nearly infinite space to fill (unless it's print, and then expect a much more rigid space restriction leading to less in the way of "human interest" stories). A good story pitch will always get some attention.

How to create a positioning statement

Create a positioning statement about your story leveraging the topics in the headlines and find will yourself alongside them in a sidebar or a related article.

Writing a powerful statement can be as easy as simply stating the issue you are addressing and why it's newsworthy in one sentence. Or, it can be a little more involved by giving examples of the issue in two or three nationally recognized situations. Weave your expertise, your personal experience, or your advocacy involvement with a respected organization or social service agency adding credibility to why YOU make a great spokesperson and then validate it for the particular venue you are pitching. For example, if you are pitching the Los Angeles Times, you should relate its importance geographically. You can do this easily by incorporating local census figures or statistics. If, again, you are pitching the Los

Angeles Times, utilize data that had appeared in their pages and source it.

The most difficult part of creating the positioning statement is not, in fact, writing it. It's editing it! Remember, think twitter. The fewer characters you present the more interest it will bring.

As an aside, you can hit two birds with one stone by starting to leave commentary in articles that tie into your story as you do your research. With the intention of weaving together a fabric of your identification to a topic or an issue, consider writing your own articles and posting them in local online venues like your local newspaper's website or patch.com. Make sure you use your name as you will in your pitch as that will also help with search engine optimization (SEO).

How to get interest in your story

Position your story for the most important and salient points. Don't get all bound up in the details as the editors will most likely cut them out anyhow. While you know there is a beginning, middle and end to your story, journalists only see the story for the important points and sometimes for the points they can sensationalize to get readership up. Those points may be completely different from the linear view of the story and if you aren't aware of that going in, you will find yourself misquoted and your story will resemble that of someone else. That kind of misunderstanding can be very painful as you are then put in a position of needing to defend a stance you didn't take rather than one that was clearly laid out from the get go.

Finding the right journalist to cover your story

My advice is always to start with a story release in a print venue. First of all, though the media reports, by the way, via the internet, that print is dead, I still see newspapers littering the coffee shops and the driveways of nearly 60% of the homes I pass as I take my kids to school at the crack of dawn. I like that major newspapers still vet all their stories through a multitude of editors adding much more credibility and integrity to your story. Vetting is when every fact and figure in the story is checked, double-checked and sometimes even triple checked for accuracy and honesty.

It may feel strange to have someone ask for proof of what you tell them, but you know they are putting their reputation and the reputation of their media venue on the line to tell your story and that should give you some peace-of-mind that it will be handled correctly. This is rarely the case in sensationalized, tabloid-esque venues that often attribute the facts to an unknown or anonymous source. Your story will work more for your mission of increasing awareness and advocacy if it's got a big name willing to stand behind it, pound a proverbial chest, and say, "I believe this to be true".

Finding the right journalist within your chosen venue is a very important step and in fact, one that is detrimental to your success in going wide with your story. Search high and low for other stories like yours. Look for the topic, where it has been covered and read those comments after the story. Look for after-stories, follow-ups and then research the blogs and websites where the story was picked up. Don't forget to look for updated information on the person who, like you aim to, told their story to see how going wide worked for them achieving their mission.

After you identify some journalists at some reputable venues, craft the one-page positioning statement you created into letter format. If you plan to send your pitch letter by email, do it in the body of the email. Never send attachments to a journalist unless they are specifically requested. It's best to be totally prepared with your sound bites, positioning statement/letter and mission before you press SEND on any email. You might be fielding a phone call and need to speak intelligibly on your pitch in a matter of minutes. The internet is the tool of immediate gratification, after all. If you do it by snail mail, wait 4 days and then follow it up with a phone call.

Remember, highlight the most important points in bullets, credit research, include if others are willing to corroborate with you in telling your story and serve as additional sources. Make it really hard for the journalist to say no to at least a brief, personal conversation with you.

What the heck is a sound bite[1]?

A sound bite is characterized by a short phrase or sentence that captures the essence of what the speaker was trying to say, and is used to summarize information and entice the reader or viewer. The term was coined by the U.S. Media in the 1970s. Due to its brevity, the sound bite often overshadows the broader context in which it was spoken, and can be misleading or inaccurate.

One of the most famous phrases in American history is an excellent example of a sound bite, "The only thing we have to fear is fear itself" delivered by Franklin D. Roosevelt in his first inaugural address. On a more recent political note, is there anyone who hasn't heard about the Mitt Romney guffaw of, "…and they brought us whole binders full of women"? So you see, sound bites can be good-memorable and bad-memorable. Tricky, right?

It's important for you to remember, and why I find it worth repeating several times in

---

[1] Listening to sound bites is both fun and can help you create them. See the Resources section for more on where to find them.

this book, that the beginning, middle and end is a linear view of your story that the journalist will most likely not be interested in.

Write your personal intro and practice your 60 second story pitch to reflect the newsworthy points that are in your positioning statement. Tie your research in. Leverage the universality of the topic and mention other high profile stories in a "ripped from the headlines" manner. Take yourself out of it other than as a credible source or witness. *You* are not what you are selling; *your story* is what you are selling.

To that end, speaking in sound bites, or small quotes that in and of themselves can stand on their own to tell the story is not easy. Remember this little ditty? "I'm going to say this again: I did not have sexual relations with that woman, Miss Lewinsky."

If you aren't careful and honest with this (remember your mission in this is your deepest truth), you will be misquoted and you will end up resentful and angry that the story told is not your own but the one the journalist wanted to tell. Remember, there are many edits between the journalist and the point in which the story appears. Also remember, you don't know the editor(s) names and they have never spoken to you, so misquoting happens a LOT!

If you misspeak, immediately correct yourself. Everyone is human and pitching a story or speaking on a live televised show can cause quite a bit of stress. Stay true to yourself and apologize for the misstep and repeat what you wanted to say.

How do you tell your story in sound bite quotes?

An excellent article on speaking in sound bites can be found on the Harvard Business School website.[2]

Here are the top points of the article entitled, "The Four Secrets to Delivering the Right Sound Bites," by Gary Genard, Harvard Management Communication Letter, 7/03.

- **Control the agenda**

Advocate rather than respond, and answer topics, not questions. Learn how to "bridge"

---

[2] http://hbswk.hbs.edu/archive/3622.html

from the question you are asked to the response you want to give.

- **Use stories, visual images, and personal examples**

Speak in ways that create visual images in listeners' minds. Enliven your point of view—and enhance your credibility—with anecdotes, personal experiences, and statistics that prove your point (although you must remember to present the statistics in human terms). Speak in ways that create visual images in listeners' minds, using simple, concrete language and, where possible, similes, metaphors, and analogies.

It's always important to remember that the journalist and the editors and the readers of your story are entitled to have a perception of reality that is perhaps the exact opposite of your truth. That's the joy of being human. We all have the right to our own opinion and our perception of what is and what isn't is based on our personal associations and experience.

Of course, all of our associations, and I do mean ALL are different based on our own life experiences. You know the saying; one man's junk is another man's treasure. It's about our associations and our life experiences. Apple pie might remind me of Thanksgiving while it might remind you of having your appendix out. It's a blue cheese kind of world, some things grow on some and some things are always just awful to others.

You must take this into consideration when you retell your story to anyone. Those that are friends might be being polite when they say they understand, when the truth is, their only association with what you tell them is what they've seen on TV or read in books. Those that don't know you won't be as kind. And, be cautious. Those that you most think will understand and support you in your retelling of your story, your family, might have a completely different retelling of the same story from their point of view.

Perspective is a thorny thing. Quantum physicists will tell you that the moment something is observed its outcome changes, merely by the existence of that observation. That tosses in variables of the nth degree as to how everyone else will hear and perceive your sound bites so make sure you practice them until you can remove most of the ambiguities. Neither you nor your observer is wrong, each just have different perceptions of reality based on the eyes that witnessed the story unfolding.

Chapter 2

Can you Plan to Go Viral?

"When you make the claim that something on the Internet is going to be good for democracy, you often [hear], 'Are you talking about the thing with the singing cats?"
Clay Shirkey, Adjunct Professor, NYU

Whether it's on your phone while you're on line at the bank or at your desk while you inhale lunch, most everybody will admit to surfing the internet aimlessly on occasion.

Most of us will hit the social sites, check out our Facebook news feeds and sometimes even "check in" at a location to let people know where we are. Perhaps we'll make a pit stop at Linked In, or we'll tweet about something we think might interest others. Or maybe, we'll wander over to look at trending topics. Headlines that scream, open me often include a celebrity name and the topic of arrest and any name that is followed by the word 'dead'. Other trending topics might drive us over to YouTube and suddenly we are watching a video that 25% of America has watched in under 8 hours.

How the heck did we (and one quarter of America) get there? And what is so special about that video that we find ourselves engaging, watching, commenting, reposting, retweeting, or blogging about it?

It's called viral video and it cuts across all vertical digital media. In other words, viral videos are those that can be posted anywhere and most often are. Viral videos are just that. Like the flu, which rips through schools and families because of its contagion factor, these videos spread like wildfire!

How do you get your story to go viral?

By creating a message that appeals to individuals with high social networking potential (and yes, I'm certain we all know social media junkies and addicts that send us viral messaging all the time) your story might potentially go viral. They are perfect targets for your viral message.

Top shelf social networkers have a high probability of sharing their communications with people they know (and don't know) within a very short period of time. So what's the right stuff to get into the right hands?

To make viral marketing work, three basic criteria must be met.

The first is that the messenger should be a marketing maven of sorts. If they are heavy in social media and have multiple neighborhoods or social hubs they "hang" at, and/or if they are salespeople (yes, your average car dealer counts!) they are your BINGO messenger. These are members of society who have their finger on the pulse of what's hot and what's not. They are often the first to know about something and they are quick to transmit it to everyone they know if they find some value in it. Think human megaphones.

The second element necessary to go viral is that your message must be memorable, engaging and interesting. If the message stirs an emotion, any emotion, AND is hinged on something memorable and interesting, you have a winner.

The third must-have is the right environment. The environment must be ideal. The timing and context of your viral message must be right. Here again, piggybacking with or spoofing a topical news item is a surefire way for your message to gain the attention of your messenger.

Creating your viral messaging

1. **Keep it current.** I covered this earlier in your positioning statement and your pitch. If the rack you can hang your story on is current and trending in the news, it's already got some stickiness. The keywords involved in your story will be top of mind as the public searches out the top national story and you will gain strength from that association. Google Trends is a great way to watch for increasing hits on specific topics and then there are the hashtags you should be alerted to.

2. **Keywords and hashtags are integral to going viral.** A hashtag, the # symbol, is used to mark keywords or topics in a Tweet and is a great way to follow trends. If a lot of people are tweeting a particular topic, there is trending in hashtag usage and it becomes a top meme. A meme, by the way is just another term for an image, video, etc. that is passed electronically from one internet user to another.

#bindersfullofwomen was a massive meme and if you spend a little time researching it on Google alone, you will find 46,000 references to it. There is no question in my mind that it hurt Romney's campaign and ticked off many voters.

Make sure your ideal phrases are in the headline, description and throughout the text. Tumblr, YouTube, and Twitter all use #hashtags so don't avoid them even if you don't 100% understand them.

3. **Get someone big to notice you!** Content often goes viral when a celebrity comes across it and shares it with their massive audience. You can tweet and blog and comment high profile celebs but there's never a guarantee they will embrace your mission or promote your story.

4. **Make a video.** The internet loves videos and viewers love to post and re-post them on their social media sites, to their blogs, websites, you name it. There are no real rules with video as top notch production is not what pushes viral activity. The best places to post your video are YouTube and Vimeo. Be thoughtful and remember once it's begun to circulate, there is

little control over where. Keep that in mind when you begin videotaping something personal.

5. **Use humor.** Parodies and spoofs often go viral on a dime. Can you make fun of yourself or the story you aim to tell? The more ridiculous the better. Buzzfeed.com is a great venue for this viral technique.

6. **Start a contest to increase traffic to your social media or web page.** A lot of social media campaigns use contests and giveaways to keep their current audience engaged and attract new people to their content. Offer up a free report on a topic relevant to your human interest story. It doesn't have to be a major piece of literature, but something that helps drive traffic.

7. **Use photos and visual content.** Catch attention with major venues like Tumblr and Pinterest which are highly visual. Facebook has even made photos bigger to view on newsfeeds as everyone realizes that with the short attention spans of the average web surfer, a

picture is worth a thousand words. (Do you like how I threw that sound bite in there?)

8. **Be shocking and/or controversial.** Strong emotions will motivate viewers to share your message to see how their friends will react about it too. Good or bad, it can still go viral!

Why some stories go viral and others don't

In a recent study[3] performed by the marketing department at The Wharton School, authors researched just why certain pieces of online content are more viral than others.

Using a unique dataset of all the New York Times articles published over a three month period, the authors examined the link between integral affect (i.e., the emotion evoked) and whether content was highly shared. Their results suggested a strong relationship between emotion and virality, but indicate that this link is more complex. Positive content was more viral (than negative content), as was content that inspired awe. But while sad content was less viral, anger or anxiety inducing articles were

---

[3] The study can be downloaded here:
http://tinyurl.com/bdydpb9

both more likely to make the paper's most emailed list. These results hold controlling for how surprising, interesting, or practically useful content is (all of which are positively linked to virality), as well as external drivers of attention (e.g., how prominently the articles were featured).

In the end, you have to accept that whether it's a result of pixie dust or just the luck of the Irish, a story that engages, enrages, or enlivens has a good shot at being in the center of a viral success story.

Chapter 3

How Do You Steer Clear of the Tabloids?

*"People who read the tabloids deserve
to be lied to."-----Jerry Seinfeld*

Ok, so let's say the journalist has reported your story and it's big but you just don't know how big, yet. There's a lot of discussion because there is emotion, controversy, a mission, and an issue bigger than you. Add to that the street cred from research and perhaps even large corporate involvement and you've got yourself big media bait. If your experience is anything like mine, it will look something like this.

You wake up the morning the article is released, which by the way, you are never quite sure of because as I mentioned before, the journalist sends it to editorial and it's out of their hands. If the paper has a holiday or shopping insert or there was some huge international political coup overnight, your story can get pushed or even perpetually shelved until a lighter news day or maybe never.

But let's say, you wake up and turn on your computer as you wipe the sleep from your eyes. You find a link to the article online from your now, rather heavily, invested journalist. You might even have a smattering of emails from friends who are earlier risers than you and found your picture on the top fold of their morning newspaper lying in the dew on their front lawn. Or maybe, you note a voice mail on your cell phone from the early birds who turned on their computer earlier than you did and came across the story online in their morning Yahoo feed.

You, no doubt, rush to click the link to read the article and either find yourself aghast at the inadequacies of the story or basking for a moment in the excitement of reaching your mission to tell your story fairly.

There is a lot to think about as you approach your day like any other, that is…until your unlisted telephone number begins to ring incessantly, the local news media camps out at the end of your driveway and the offers for all accommodations paid boondoggles start piling up as the talk show producers in different time zones begin to scour the wire for the next BIG story.

Preparing for the onslaught of TV reporters competing for an exclusive scoop

Well, don't do what I did. After dropping the kids off at school, I went to a friend's house and hid in her basement in avoidance and denial of the attention. I sat with her and her incredibly sick 4 year old daughter until I felt like I could face the onslaught of attention from the 750 word article and half page four color picture of our family that appeared above the fold on tens of thousands of driveways and news boxes throughout Chicago land. I just plain ignored the 27 voice mail messages that had piled up. Add to that the emails adding up to over 700 over the course of the following two days and of course the impending US Mail that would fill the box with emotional support, threats and name calling.

On a more immediate level, I had CNN, ABC and NBC all vying to get our family on an exclusive morning show appearance. Some only wanted us if we would bring our daughter. Each one had invasive requests in order to create an exclusive that would one-up the print media. Bring the child, bring the family, pictures of the now deceased birthmother. You name it. Nothing was beyond request no matter how inappropriate. Forget medical confidentiality, they wanted to interview the doctors directly. They wanted details, as yet untold, and they wanted them to be juicy. They were going to squeeze the life out of this story.

More to the point of my denial in the basement, all of them wanted an answer NOW and when they didn't get it, they followed with 6 or more voice mails AND emails. Some resorted to calling my mother (whose married name is different than even my maiden name) and alerting her to the need to reach me before she even knew about the article. There was drama and frenetic chaos all over this story. The public was enraged at me. The media wanted to coddle me.

By the following morning, I had chosen GMA because of its integrity. I trusted George Stephanopoulos and Robin Roberts and they weren't looking for gory, juicy details. They agreed to block our daughter's face to protect her anonymity and they took no for an answer when we refused to bring the kids or the guardians. They didn't buy us a fancy boondoggle and that showed respect for what really mattered. Plus, they had covered a few other stories on FASD and I respected their intent to do what was right to bring attention to the matter. They would most certainly give me the opportunity to send a message of prevention. Literally 7 hours after I made the commitment to an exclusive and said no to the others, Oprah's producers called and called and called.

What I learned through my experience in this part of the process is, go with your gut. We made the right choice and I never questioned it. Even AFTER spending the 7 months that followed telling the ongoing saga to the Oprah producer I came to call a supportive friend.

Over a year later she would call to offer us an appearance on a show that just didn't sound right at the outset. As it turned out, the show ended up being about 'Kids Who Kill'. As much as the producer was charged to get us on the show, she tried selling me out of the idea when she called to alert me to the opportunity.

Instinctively I knew she would be much more excited if she felt it was the right opportunity. Her friendship was worth more to me than telling our story on Oprah, especially when it became clear that they needed to one-up GMA by insisting we allow Oprah to visit with our daughter in her guardian's home. The media didn't care if they compromised the solution that supported our family. Hey, a story is a story and ratings are all that matter.

Teasing out the sensationalizer's that are promising to turn you into a celebrity

Keep your eye on the ball. Be prepared for other media venues to approach you after your story is released in print. Visit the websites of those shows, research other stories they have done. If they are covering stories by poking the protagonists in the sides steer clear of them. If you are offered first class airfare, fancy hotels, meals and all accommodations in a hotel you normally couldn't afford, be cautious. If after speaking to one producer, you get calls from multiple producers from the same location to unearth additional as-yet-untold scoop, be aware. What you say matters. Everything is a sound bite. Whether it's a direct quote or just an assertion, the visual version of your story will flow with their first impressions.

Take your time making a choice. If they are rushing you, just consider how much they want the story. They are rushing you because if you commit to them you won't be able to back out if you get a better offer. Lastly, if they offer to pay you, give you a book deal or offer to connect you with a film company, run - don't walk!

Again, I chose GMA based on its viewership and its overall integrity. That said, I also had 20+ years of marketing know-how to help me recognize what to look for to meet my personal mission.

Would Ellen have been an equally good choice? Yes, but her producers missed the article. Would Ricki Lake have been an option? Maybe. The audience would have been a little younger and perhaps not mature enough to recognize the selflessness of parenting, though binge drinking in younger women is very common, with research to support, and often pregnancy is the unplanned outcome of a binge drinking episode. When it was all said and done, those two shows weren't in the mix of dueling talk shows wanting us to appear but that is how you should consider the media that approach you. Do *you* watch their shows? Do you fit in the target audience that would benefit the most from hearing your story? Put on that hat and try that venue on for size.

Whatever you do, I suggest not selling your soul for your 15 minutes of fame. This is what I meant when I said understand your mission. If your mission is ego-centric, consider how you will be viewed by others after the energy behind your story settles down to a simmer again. If you have children, consider how their lives will be affected if you appear on Jerry Springer and get humiliated as Jerry pokes at your integrity by bringing up some skeleton in your closet. Judge your choices this way. If the show's website has a promotion for episodes titled *Sister Smackdown* or *I had a baby with a Tranny*, then say no and have faith you made the right decision.

Lastly, not long after GMA, the tabloids from Europe contacted me. I'm not talking tabloids like the New York Post, I'm talking about the paper with the un-vetted front page story about the 65 year old mother who was inseminated with her daughter's egg and her son-in-law's sperm so she could give birth to their baby. International fame in this manner is not hard won, but your reputation might as well be after you say yes. Consider offers like this thoroughly before you even return the phone call of interest. Have the journalist send you clips from previous stories he or she has written. If any of it sounds like it could have been torn from the pages of the Enquirer, I think you have your answer.

The, as yet, untold details of your story

The talk/news shows and even radio interviewers are going to want something different from the print version of your story. They are going to want the "as yet untold" details of your story and you will need to decide how much you want to share in order to support your mission. You must be very cognizant of protecting other's rights to their personal privacy.

In our case, as a family, we decided that helping to prevent FASD was worth being judged by those that didn't understand our personal and tragic story. As much as they would have loved to see video of our daughter in an active raging tantrum or pictures of what she looked like grown up rather than just baby pictures, GMA respected our right to respect our daughter's privacy and the integrity of her placement with a family that deserved complete anonymity.

Our daughter knew that I had been both blogging and writing a book about parenting her for nearly two years before she left our family home. I would never have written about her nor have divulged what was happening behind our white picket fence unless she was ok with it. Granted, she was 6 and 7 and pretty unstable at the time, but she was well aware that sharing our story would help other children not have to struggle like she did. She is a brave and selfless soul that I have respect and unconditional love for. It's important to know where your priorities are before you decide you want to be the news.

The interesting thing is that the ongoing commentary on the clip of our nearly 2 year old segment on GMA and the accompanying ABC News story is much less judgmental than the commentary on the original print story from the same time period. An obvious outcropping of the way the story was positioned. Again, something that I learned after the fact in our case, and something that I can teach you before you approach the media.

Turn back to the salient points of your story. If you had 5 to start with but only 3 got sufficiently covered in your original print article, pull out the other 2 and assess if they are still important topics. Then, offer those up as new details that haven't been released yet. They make your story that much more attractive to the media and you are not divulging anything beyond what you planned to when you first set out on your mission to tell your story.

Avoiding the stupid human tricks that some talk show hosts will try to coax you with

Just say no. Be gracious and express humility for the opportunity they are giving you to tell your story, but don't do anything you have to think about twice.

Live talk shows can be very anxiety producing. Do your best to get a sense for their line of questioning before you sit in front of their cameras. In some cases, they will actually give you the questions ahead of time. They might even do an off-camera practice interview with you to give you a sense for how it will happen.

Try not to squirm. Take a nice deep cleansing breath before you begin to speak. Remember your goal and just relax in knowing you are telling a story that will mean something to a subset of the audience watching you and nothing to another subset. Some will judge, some will not. Some will support, some will forget, others will bring it up over dinner with friends. Some will post it on social media, others will post comments based on guttural responses.

Starting a national conversation is not about the stupid human tricks that will set you apart from everyone else. Starting a national conversation is a way to direct energy and attention, both positive and negative, towards an issue you care deeply about. Look your interviewer in the eye when you answer their questions and don't be tempted to go off-topic. Just go with what your gut instinct tells you to do, even if the host goes in a direction you hadn't originally discussed.

An appropriate response for an interviewer or host that goes off script with a question is, "Hmmm. I hadn't expected you to ask that question so I'm really not prepared to answer it" or…if you are prepared, you can shock the interviewer with, "I'm so glad you asked that. I was afraid you might not."

My last word on this subject is, don't compromise your integrity. Stand by your story, your truth, your perception of reality and your mission. Be consistent. Be grateful for the opportunity to speak to so many at once about a subject you care so deeply about and know that in some small way, this story happened to you for exactly this reason; so you could help nudge our species towards being a more kind and loving neighbor to those that need our attention.

Chapter 4

Who's Entitled to an Opinion?

"There are in fact two things, science and opinion; the former begets knowledge, the latter ignorance." ----- Hippocrates

opin ion (as defined by Merriam Webster)

noun

1. a view, judgment, or appraisal formed in the mind about a particular matter

2. belief stronger than impression and less strong than positive knowledge

Like fingerprints, there are trillions of opinions belonging to millions of people and every one of them is their perception of someone else's reality. Choosing to go wide with your story and be the news opens you up to all manner of repercussions from those people.

Finding out who your friends and supporters are is often a disarming and eye opening experience. The outcome of telling your story will be full of surprises and the temptation to confront those that shock you with a lack of support is one you need to step back from.

In her book aptly named, *Coping With Infuriating, Mean, Critical People: The Destructive Narcissistic*, author Nina Brown writes, "Having opinions differs in degree from being opinionated. The first allows for differing points of view, the second does not. One who has opinions can also keep their mind open for new information and this allows for the possibility of change. One who is opinionated is just the opposite. No new information will be considered and there is no possibility for change of perspective."

Acceptance is said to be the first step of self discipline and you will need to practice much self discipline as you see others creating opinions and reacting to both your story and whatever level of "celebrity" you earn by going wide.

There will be disbelief, denial, grief, and anger that could even resemble rage towards you. A veritable buffet of human emotion could evolve from friends, acquaintances, family, strangers-you name it. And you must practice self discipline and find strength in knowing your story is yours. Your experience and your perception of reality is yours. Own it no matter what others think or say.

Brown continues, "While mostly everyone doesn't want to be considered wishy-washy or unable to form an opinion, most of us do want to be flexible and outgoing. The opinionated person is difficult to interact with because there is no possibility that anyone else's perspective will be considered. Destructive narcissists can be extremely opinionated, refusing to entertain any new perspectives, facts or opinions of others. The mere suggestion that they may be in error is enough to enrage or provoke attacks on others."

Welcome to the world of anonymity

In 1993, during the web's infancy, the New Yorker printed a very fitting cartoon with one mutt saying to another, "On the Internet, nobody knows you're a dog." It became an emblem of that freedom and, for years, it was the magazine's most reproduced cartoon. Since then, some news sites like the New York Times and the Washington Post among others have revised their policies regarding anonymous comments.

Arianna Huffington, founder of The Huffington Post says that anonymity is just the way things are done. "It's an accepted part of the internet, but there's no question that people hide behind the anonymity to make vile or controversial comments."

The debate over anonymity is entwined with the question of giving more weight to comments from some readers than from others, based in part on how highly other readers regard them. Some sites already use a version of this approach and it works sometimes, but not all the time.

Here is an excerpt from a serial anonymous commentator who writes me regularly. He or she is very angry at their own perception of me in every way and yet regularly visit my blog to attack my character.

"Your family is dysfunctional because of you and your choices. It was never about your daughter. All of your pretty prose and alternate profanity can not cover the fact that you are deeply, deeply disturbed. Nobody wants to read about how you used and then abandoned that baby girl. What are you going to do now that she is gone? Who will be your scapegoat now?"

And this one from the Chicago Tribune article,

"Her husband should divorce the piece of sh*t. Only Satan would throw away a child like that!"

When I look at the commentary on any article I am often left wondering if the majority of viewers have any reading comprehension whatsoever. Or worse, do readers only glance at the first few paragraphs of a news story and make an inference as to what the article is about from the comments before they apply their slanderous pen?

There is something to be said for your trumpeteers though. Especially when they start a comment "war" in which they pick up their wordsmithing weapons and fight a battle for your honor. If you do take time to look at the commentary for your pickups, note the dynamic interplay between the two types of readers. It's a wonderful study in human psychology.

If there is someone deeply important to you that could be harmed in any way by telling your story, talk to them before you pick up your megaphone. Forgiveness may be hard won.

This is the hard and true potential downfall of dedicating yourself to a mission that means something to you, and is almost always the reason that many decide not to go public with their story in the hopes someone *else* will become their spokesperson instead.

Make a list of those closest to you that may fall prey to judgmental commentators speak to every single one of them about the potential pitfalls of promoting your human interest story, BEFORE you reach out to even one journalist.

Next, attempting to respond to haters and judgers is fruitless. Move on. Keep a healthy outlook.

Unless someone ties the shoelaces on your shoes and then walks a mile, they wouldn't have the slightest idea what it was like to live your story. Defensiveness and attentiveness to their commentary works against the strong positioning you have in your mission so to quote a famous First Lady, "Just Say No" to defending your position and your actions. Healthy debate is good. Let the national discussion ensue.

"Criticism may not be agreeable, but it is necessary. It fulfills the same function as pain in the human body. It calls attention to an unhealthy state of things."----- Winston Churchill

Everyone loves a critic

Everyone loves a critic? Really? I beg to differ.

If you are ready for the part that cuts to the bone, and can't help but look out of curiosity, start reading the commentary on your story. If not, wait at least a year before you look at the disturbing amount of negativity there is in the world. By then, you will either be past personalizing it or, like me and deep into therapy.

Use our story as an example.

I have links for the articles on my blog (www.gertz-pileofideas.blogspot.com). Just surf down to the comments and hang on, especially to those that appeared after our Chicago Tribune article that was edited to the topic rather than the integrity of the story. It was definitely someone else's perception of the reality that was our story. Specifically, it was an editor twice or three times removed from the journalist that spent 8 weeks and countless hours with me detailing the timeline of events as they happened. As such, the comments reflected the story not "as told by" Lori Gertz or even "as told by" the reporter, but "as told by" the Chicago Tribune editor who was the last person to give a slant and headline to the piece and someone I never met at all.

The frightening power of a pajama clad commentator

I have always accepted that everyone has a right to their own opinion and when there is debate there is a healthy discourse-whether or not we agree in the end. Any discussion is good discussion. Akin to any press being good press if what you want to do is start a national debate about something that is important to you.

If in the end of that discourse, we still don't come to terms on our opinions, I accept that we disagree and I move on grateful for the opportunity to have been able to air my opinion and hear yours. But criticism by someone that isn't brave enough to put their name after it just isn't valid in my book. There is no courage in anonymity as it pertains to name-calling and rage-filled personal attacks.

Some news sites do review comments after they are posted, but most say they do not have the resources to do routine policing. Many sites allow readers to flag objectionable comments for removal, and make some effort to block comments from people who have repeatedly violated the site's standards so there is some effort to cleaning up the attacks.

The truth is, when commentators are asked to provide their real names for display online, most give false identities anyhow. And lets be honest, verifying them would be too labor-intensive to be realistic for anyone to take on. Most news venues feel that merely making the demand for a name and an e-mail address weeds out much of the most offensive commentary, but that wasn't my experience.

Hundreds of news stories and editorials compare the Internet to the "Wild West," some to illustrate the opportunities available in cyberspace, but most warn of its dangers. I get it. I've been bullied behind its barely regulated walls. It's a wide open space where anyone can say anything to and about anyone and do so behind the curtain of anonymity quite easily.

That said, the internet's rise has fueled the pajama clad commentator and the nasty, sometimes slanderous and vilifying comments they leave hang out there like yesterday's dirty laundry. And they do hang out there. In fact, those comments hang out there in perpetuity fueling discussion for a very long time.

Chapter 5

Be Careful What You Wish For

"Nothing that goes on in anyone else's mind can harm you."-----Marcus Aurelius

Perpetuity- Your story and the power of the internet and beyond

When you think about it, the concept of 'forever' is grossly overrated.

The idea that our words and actions will survive our own date with mortality and live on in perpetuity is the foundation that the internet is built on. Hell hath no fury like a resentful flame posting untrue rumors about you or worse inappropriate photos. Consider how a potential employer might react when stumbling upon these embarrassing crumbs of immature youth and you will scratch the itch of understanding what forever can mean as it relates to your human interest story on the internet.

While I live by the words of Aurelius and Terry Cole-Whitaker's "what you think of me is none of my business", following my heart and mission has certainly made it challenging to maintain my own anonymity and manage my reputation, be it professional or personal. The truth is that the unintended outcomes of media attention include assumptions about you that may not be true based on the comments and storylines that follow the release of your story to the media.

I am certainly no stranger to reverse online reputation tactics and have been hired many times to help clients regain their strength online after a particularly destructive ex-employee or disgruntled customer posted nasty comments about them. I, had however never been the target before our story was caught in the national spotlight.

You might be crucified or you might become a media darling. It's a crapshoot. I was vilified (interestingly my husband got off scot-free) and handling it with grace continues to be a deep learning experience for me.

The cherry on the sundae is that the misquoting, the on-target points, and all the commentary all continue to sit out there in a virtual wonderland of information.

It's dizzying to consider how many pickups your story will have once it hits the wire. Ours had over 10,000 locations on the net when first reported, and today there are over 153,000 locations where my name and my daughter's name reside together just with a name search.

With each location the story appeared, there were both supportive and earsplitting attacks on us, my character and the system sometimes numbering in the hundreds.

Maintaining a sense of proportion as it relates to the number of eyeballs that see it is nearly impossible. Not only will they see your story when it is reported but they will still be able to see it long after you are pushing daisies. The upside of course, is with that, you are closer to realizing your mission.

Your reputation – preparing for the upshot of being in the national spotlight

One must remember that what another says of you is a reflection of how they see themselves. In my case, the Sophie's choice of how to keep all of my children safe from harm, or what I call my dark night of the soul, was too much for other, mostly mothers, to consider. No doubt, every parent has a moment when they look at their child raising experience as something other than what they idealized.

Perhaps, if we are being really straightforward with one another, as parents of special needs kids often are, there are moments when we think we can't do it another moment.

My honesty and my final determination that I just couldn't keep my daughter safe anymore and someone else could surely do it better was about me saving her life and the lives of my other children, not about giving up so I could go have my nails done. I don't need to argue that point with anyone, no less someone who hasn't played a role in my human interest story and who has just damned me to hell because of the article title the editor decided would get the most 'views'.

My name, for example, can be found and associated to pick-your-poison reputation killers like "America's most hated mother" or "the mother that threw her child away". It can sometimes take pages or even searching my maiden name to uncover proof of my 26 year marketing career in multiple publishing venues, my successful woman-owned business, or any of the articles I have had published.

Ego surf your name now, before you go decide to be the news. Keep a finger on the pulse of your reputation by regular Google alerts with your name, as well as the key words from your story's topic hot-buttons and remember to comment carefully.

Consider hiring a reputation management firm (I've posted a list in the resource section) if things get out of control. It worked for BP after that little matter of the oil spill, right?

Getting back to your mission statement

How you'll utilize the media attention to leverage an ongoing position of advocacy or awareness depends on your stamina and tolerance.

You are assigned to guest blog as much as you can. Write articles about your story monthly if not bi-weekly. Keep tying them into newsworthy happenings in the world. Place them or links to them on highly ranked sites.

Another tactic that is equally as effective is to find new stories with common topics on which to comment and include a link to your article in the commentary.

Set up a Facebook page for your efforts and collect "likes" by promoting your mission to all of your friends and business associates if it is appropriate. Use that venue as a means to post new articles of interest that you have written or that have been written about your story as it begins to grow tentacles.

The reason for all the social media activity is two-fold. The first reason is to keep your story and your efforts top of mind. When you post the links to the media coverage you garner (sensationalized titles or otherwise), comment on articles of interest and send new readers to your media coverage links you are keeping your material at the top of the search engine.

The second reason goes along with that because if you are at the top of the search engine on your name and story search, then your commentators with any negative hubbub are not.

The best way to manage your reputation is to push down any negative comments associated with your name. That's pretty much what those reputation firms do anyhow. Of course, they are programmers and know the tricks to backlinks, linkwheels and pyramids of search engine optimization that I won't go into here for fear of sending most of you screaming from this book. Hire them if your efforts aren't working well enough to get what *you* want on the top of the first page of your ego-surfing.

Most business prospects do a Google search before they retain my company and often times they will find my personal story. While I have worked tirelessly to push the comments down, the story has staying power and every time there is a similar story, or most recently a tragedy of huge proportions relating to a mentally unstable child, I become the media's go-to-gal for sound bites and contacts with other families like mine.

I am an all "out there" kind of person. I always have been. As such, I am the sum of my experiences and so I have accepted that if a potential client or employer thinks I am deserved of vilification then we won't have the kind of working relationship I would strive for anyhow. In a way, having our story hanging out there on the internet in perpetuity is a little like a litmus test for who will be a long term relationship and who will be a fly-by.

I am blessed with an incredible support system in my Facebook community and blog readership and rarely feel pummeled by the commentators anymore. That doesn't mean the haters have stopped though, and I'm glad they haven't. As long as they are out there swingin' at me, there is a national discussion. And of course, as long as there is a national discussion, I'm happy to have gone wide with my story.

Epilogue

Our Story

"The study of stories people tell about their lives is no longer a promising new direction for personality psychology. Instead, personal narratives and the life story have arrived." -----
Daniel P. McAdams

As I mentioned earlier in the book, ours is a story that had a pretty linear timeline and began with a private adoption. Many people assumed at first that it was an adoption story but it was never an adoption story, though I came to live our story because we adopted. I am a huge proponent of adoption and I have never changed my positioning on it. I place blame on no one. Our story is *our* story. Our adoption, and only our adoption, was sadly built on a foundation of deceit.

Perhaps for all the right reasons, our daughter's birthmother chose to hide her prenatal abuse in order to find the best family for her baby. Her mindset was, no doubt, that the right family could undo any of the harm she caused to the baby by her drug and alcohol abuse, no less her own psychological problems. The trouble started when she didn't tell us about that abuse. We had a long row to hoe to find out what was the cause of our daughter's difficulties. That said, along we came eager to adopt her as-yet unborn baby girl.

Did being told that she only smoked one cigarette a day throughout her pregnancy help us to make a decision? You bet. Had we been told otherwise, would we still have adopted her? You bet. We never knew what we didn't know to know. The moral of our story is that unconditional love is just that. You do what is best for your children because you love them unconditionally. That includes letting them go, whether or not they have reached the prime age of 18.

After a series of events that left the integrity of our entire family in the balance, we were forced into creating a band-aid solution. The failings of the mental health system for our "fall-through-the-crack-kid" kept on keeping on, and no matter how many agencies I turned to for help, the one asset we actually owned outright (our car) meant we didn't meet the requirements for support. No village. No hammock. No respite. Just a 12 inch pile of lost therapeutic hope, doctors without suggestions, schools without security or peace of mind for her safety, insurance that wouldn't recognize her impaired reality or her need for long-term care, and danger in every corner of our home.

This was our life. Our daughter needed to be with others struggling with FASD, not swimming upstream against the tide of other more recognizable disabilities. She needed to be in a home without the demands of emotional reciprocation not in ours where she resented the developmental norms and responsibilities of living in a nuclear family. At points I didn't know what needed more attention, her reactive attachment disorder from the adoption trauma, the increasing mania from her bipolar disorder or her organic brain damage from alcohol exposure. All were huge topics of controversy everywhere I looked to educate myself.

How did our news attract attention?

A solution born of years of research and a very long-term relationship with a Neuro-Developmental specialist, we very thoughtfully and carefully arranged to get her settled in a special private school and a stipend-for-board housing situation with a family experienced in foster and attachment care. Three days after she left us we heard she was calling them mommy and daddy; a slap to the face of any parent no less one that had devoted every day of 7 years and nearly every penny we had to parenting her.

A week after she had left our home to live across the country, I contacted a reporter I have great respect for at the Chicago Tribune. The journalist had previously covered a number of stories about children and families struggling with mental health issues and specifically with issues related to exposure to drugs and alcohol in-utero.

I detailed the tragedy of us having to send our child out-of-state because the state of Illinois had nothing for her and within our story she identified some very salient and topical newsworthy points.

Just 4 months before, a Tennessee-based adoptive mother of a child from Russia stuck a "return to sender" note in his pocket and put him on a flight to Russia alone when she found his continued oppositional behavior unmanageable and was denied public assistance with him.

Her story was masked in all kinds of gray areas like living in a walled compound, home schooling him versus tapping public schools and services and having only approached her mother for support in raising him. Her behavior was seen as a travesty and she was judged guilty before she was even "charged" because of the seemingly uncaring and neglectful way she addressed the matter. Her actions resulted in a short-term halt on some Russian adoptions and increasingly poor relations with Russian officials. (See recent stories relating to The Ranch in Montana known as a short-term residential home to many Russian adoptees diagnosed with FASD)

The woman in Tennessee just became unwilling and unable to parent her son any longer. Did I judge her? No. Do I condone what she did? No. Did I see a common thread in our stories? Sadly, there were some commonalities but the media saw more. But, and this is a big BUT, were our stories the same? Absolutely not. Despite the differences in the stories, the common threads made our story that much more attractive to the media. Suddenly I was not fighting an uphill battle to be heard like I had been for the 7 years prior.

Suddenly I had the story-du-jour and everyone wanted a taste.

Every journalist loves a great scoop

What made our story most attractive was transparency where in Tennessee there were secrets.

Our story appeared very similar on some important points, in more than one way, to the one that made headlines but there was more information. No secrets. No skeletons. There was adoption, but there was no abandonment; there was further proof that the system wasn't equipped to handle situations like these. And maybe, just maybe, these situations weren't as isolated as one would initially assume.

As it turned out, for decades Custody Relinquishment had been the dirty secret for failed adoptions due to reactive attachment disorder and unmanageable behavioral difficulties and not in isolated cases. By 2009[1], there were custody relinquishment cases numbering in the tens of thousands. (See GAO 2003 Report[2])

Ours wasn't a story of custody relinquishment, though many of those stories have never been acknowledged publicly. Sadly, parents are left feeling so much shame and guilt for being unable to find solutions for kids (adopted or biological) they love unconditionally but cannot keep safe in their homes, they move and change their names to avoid the judgment of others. It's hard to stand up and tell your story and not be swayed by public opinion.

I had worked tirelessly and very publicly looking for support and resources to help me care for my daughter. We took a second mortgage and eventually lost our home as I spent money I didn't have looking for any therapy that might help our little girl find some sense of peace.

Her behavior was a true aberration to anything I (and most of our doctors and therapists) had ever seen no less imagined. There was just no consistent learned behavior, no understanding of cause and effect and no boundaries. Her rage was unparalleled and her self destructive tendencies were gaining strength over what common sense she had as such a young child. Her modus operandi became suicide as she celebrated her 6th birthday and she ran into traffic and chaotic parking lots along with jumping out of moving vehicles. I couldn't keep her or anyone in our family safe anymore and no one in Illinois could help me.

The media megaphone

The journalist who took on the project did so with a full commitment to tell the entire story, highlighting the significant points about the increase in fetal alcohol spectrum disorder, the lack of recognition of the disorder in the medical field, and the black hole of support services and funding to help those raising kids born with it (an invisible disability until the oppositional behavior makes itself the elephant in the room).

She spoke to national organizations, physicians and local service organizations who had failed to provide us with the support that would have eliminated the need for us to move her from our home. She pulled quotes where she could get them from agencies that had heard our story but were still unable to provide resources.

The story she wrote had feeling. It had a beginning, middle and end and throughout it she wove research and proven facts to support the statements inherent in my sound bites. Although I was able to provide proof and confirm information when she was finished, I had absolutely no control over the final content of the article. Nor did she. Once it was on her editor's desk, it was out of her hands.

My mission throughout was to increase awareness of FASD and help other families avoid what we had to resort to. I hoped that by pointing the finger at the failings of our educational and state mental health systems that it would effect some change for others struggling with the same challenges.

It was unacceptable to me that as a taxpaying citizen I could not get one ounce of support for my daughter. It was also a rude awakening that the hammock we have all been led to believe serves as the mental health system in our country is nearly nonexistent.

I have no doubt that the journalist also had a personal mission of high standards, which is why I contacted her to begin with. I had also contacted a few others that had covered the topic but eventually chose to give her an exclusive when it became clear the story would get wider distribution in my state, where at the very least, I hoped that the administrators and politicians who had failed my family would find themselves wiping egg off their faces.

The post-mortem of a media frenzy

I have learned much from this experience of moving from a private citizen to a national advocate for the awareness of a disability that stems from a very controversial act of a mother-to-be.

I met my mission after appearing on Good Morning America and promoting the message of FASD prevention to over six million viewers. Those six million viewers and potential parents were in addition to those that read our story in any of the 153,000 pickups over the wire both in the US and overseas. Ours was one of the top read stories that year in the Chicago Tribune and the firestorm of commentary put it in the Top Ten most commented stories in the Tribune, ever. But the work of spreading the word, whether it be by telling our story or educating youth about the dangers of drinking while pregnant, is never done.

No matter its outcome to me or our family personally, if telling our story gets just one mother to put down the glass of wine or whiskey sour and step away from the bar, it saves one baby from the legacy of brain damage from prenatal exposure. And that is rewarding in and of itself. Education is the only way to FASD prevention. The choice must be the mother's. Speaking out is also a way to call attention to the fact that situations like ours are not just isolated incidents. The more stories like mine that are told, the more likely the controversy will lead to funding, programming and change!

Creating a national discussion is the best way to effect change. As I said at the beginning of this book, being at the center of that discussion is not an easy place to sit, but well worth the outcome!

---

[1] Relinquishing Custody-The tragic result of the failure to meet children's mental health Needs– Source: Bazelon Center for mental Health Law

[2] "Some officials estimate that parents relinquished over 12,700 children to state or federal custody to access mental health services" Source GAO Report 2003

Resources

- How to Write a Press Release
- How to Create Your Own Media List
- Sources for Finding Media Contacts
- Research Resources
- Sound Bites
- Reputation Management Companies
- Why Free Press Release Services Work
- 5 Ways Free Press Release Sites Can Cost You
- A Sampling of Good Free Press/Media Release Distribution Websites
- The Top Paid Press/Media Release Distribution Websites
- Great Tools to Track Your Footprints on the Internet

How to Write a Press Release

Publicity is supposedly seven times more effective than advertising, and it is free if you do it yourself! Learn how to write a press release to capture the attention of journalists, and you can cash in on the free editorial coverage.

Identify your Unique Selling Proposition?

The first and most important thing is to have something interesting to say. Consider your unique selling proposition (USP) or as I like to call it your point of differentiation. Just like in sales, you are selling a story idea to the media. So it really needs to shimmer and be compelling, more than simply an advertisement or a humdrum product plug.

Another element to consider to really hook the journalist in is the emotional selling point (ESP). Often it is the human interest element of the story that will capture attention. What is your background? Have you overcome any obstacles to get where you are today? What are your achievements or milestones?

Benefits, Benefits, Benefits

When planning how to write a press release, you need to make it clear how your product or service will benefit others.

"Small to mid size businesses now have a better way to measure, monitor and manage the costs involved in running their business, thanks to Gradich's new online measurement and analysis accounting system" sounds a lot more interesting than "Gradich Accountants today announced the launch of their revolutionary new accountancy software package..."

How to Write the Header

Write a concise but catchy headline that will grab the reader's attention. Research titles in newspapers and magazines to get ideas for headers. If you are planning to email your release, the same principles apply. Use a compelling, proactive subject heading or the journalist will delete it without even opening it.

Writing the Body of the Release

Start with a strong, compelling lead paragraph. You only have a few seconds to grab their attention, don't waste it on boring, lengthy copy. It helps to consider the 5 W's – Who, What, When, Where, Why but don't forget the zip.

Don't forget to highlight the benefit to the reader and perhaps include some "how to" tips relating to your product or service. Throw in a few memorable quotes, either from yourself or someone well-known who can endorse your product so it can make the story seem more real or human. A good quote can include why you've started your business or developed your product or how it helps your target audience.

Formatting your Release to Make it Sing

Title your document "Media Release" or "For Immediate Release" and include the date and your contact details, including telephone, mobile, email and website address.

Use letterhead or paste your logo on to the top of the page and keep it to one page. That is the industry standard. When using email, cut and paste into the body of the email, don't send an attachment or the chances are it won't be opened.

Who Will You Send It To?

As well as knowing how to write a media release, you also need to know who to send it to. Be sure to do your research and find out the name and direct email address of the most appropriate person. Make sure the music editor is still just that and not now the theater editor. In this world of cutbacks, sometimes the same editor writes for different parts of the paper. Do your research carefully. Editor's don't take too kindly to having a pitch sent to everyone on staff. They do have regular meetings to compare notes, so make sure you are pitching your release to the most targeted list.

Follow Up and Follow Through

Always follow up with a phone call or email and keep your media contacts consistent. If you provide good information you are not a nuisance, you are providing a service. Journalists and editors need our stories to fill their newspapers, magazines and radio shows.

An added benefit to supply is a photo; or you can suggest a photo opportunity that will add to the impact of having your story picked up.

Knowing how to write a press release will help you gain publicity, awareness and become known as an expert in your business field. This is a great way to enhance your reputation and help your business grow!

For more information on how to write a press or news release for distribution, go to: www.squidoo.com/how-to-write-a-press-release-or-news-release. There you will find 15 e-books written by accredited public relations pros guiding you through the writing and distribution process.

How to Create Your Own Media List

1. Decide which media outlets you want to target. You probably wouldn't pitch a story about senior citizens to an alternative rock radio station. Choose the media that will have an interest in your story.

2. Go to the web site for each media outlet. Most have a "Contact Us" page, but do not send your story idea to a general contact email address.

3. Look for an editor, producer or reporter and find their email address. Often, you will find it on a profile page for the person, or on a page with a story they did. Tip: You may have greater success contacting an editor or producer than a reporter.

4. If you can't find an email address for a specific person, try using the organization's default email structure. Most companies use a standard format for employees at their company email addresses. For example, first.last@media.com, firstlast@media.com, or

firstinitallast@media.com. If you want to reach reporter Jim Smith, but can't find his email address, see what the structure is for other employees there. Then, use that structure for Jim. If the addresses you found were first.last@media.com you'll probably have very good luck with jim.smith@media.com.

5. Consider buying a list of media contacts. There are sources where you can buy a list of media email addresses and other contact information. If you want to reach a lot of media outlets, or can't find contacts for the ones you want, buying a list might be the best way to go.

Good Tips to Remember

- Keep your pitches short and to the point. Never deluge your contact.
- Put all information in the body of an email. Never use attachments.
- Never spam media outlets. Send personal pitches to each contact.

Sources for Finding Media Contacts

Geographic list of US Newspapers:
http://www.usnpl.com

100 Top Television Markets:
http://www.stationindex.com/tv/tv-markets

Purchase a Customized Media Contacts List:
http://publicitycontacts.com/custom-media-contacts-list

Regional and Local Magazine List:
http://bookmarketingbestsellers.com/regional-and-local-magazines/

Research Resources

Education and Organizations Resource Directory:
http://wdcrobcolp01.ed.gov/Programs/ERO D/

Encyclopedia of Associations:
http://www.infoplease.com/ipa/A0004878.ht ml

Search/keywords to search to find additional resources to support your story:

- List of professional associations in United States
- US trade associations list
- directory of trade associations
- encyclopedia of associations
- list of business associations in the us
- largest us associations
- association list

Sound Bites

Hark.com. Hark is the world's platform for sound bites, where users can discover, create, play and share their favorite audio moments anywhere on any device through digital embedding, or via social networks such as Facebook, Twitter or Google+. Hark is the top ranking, independent entertainment website on the Internet (ComScore, 2012).

Reputation Management Companies

Top 10 Reputation Management Companies (listed in order) as chosen by Visibility, the Magazine for Online Marketing Strategies (tinyurl.com/avg8p)

- Reputationchanger.com
- ReputationManagementConsultants.com
- Netmark.com
- Customermagnetism.com
- Brucelay.com
- 1SEO.com
- Rebuildmyreputation.com
- SEOimage.com
- Submit-express.com
- Iprospect.com

Why Free Press Release Services Work

With a well-written, newsworthy press release, you can:

1) **Distribute your press release globally**, and almost immediately (pending the editor's review and approval process).

2) **Boost social buzz** with tweets, Facebook "likes," Google+ fans, and LinkedIn business connections. Many press release services allow readers to share your press release with simple social media tools.

3) **Increase traffic to your website or blog.** Your press release can persuade and engage the reader so they visit your website.

4) **Build backlinks** for your website. You can include links and/or contextual links within your press release that link directly back to your website. 5) **Complement your existing marketing campaigns**. A press release or a series of them that span many months can work jointly with other types of marketing, such as article distribution and social networking

6) **Improve your website's Page Rank** (PR)4. A press release that keeps building diverse backlinks will improve your PR. The higher your website's page rank, the more frequent it will appear in search engine results.

7) **Rank higher** in Google, Bing, Yahoo! and other search engines. Quality (diverse) backlinks plus high PageRank equals ranking higher in search engine results, above your competitors.

8) **Create viral marketing**. Although this is better won in other techniques, a well-written press release that appeals greatly to readers can create a "snowball effect," in which readers keep sharing your press release with more readers with no stop in sight.

---

[4] **PageRank**: Google uses a "secret" metric formula to analyze the credibility, popularity and "trust" of a website. This is called a PageRank. It ranks from 0 to 10 (with 10 being the highest). The most important component that adds to the strength of a PageRank is the number of quality backlinks from other websites.

5 Ways Free Press Release Sites Can Cost You $$$

--An excerpt from an article that you can read in full here: http://www.30minutepr.com/5-ways-free-press-release-sites-can-cost-you/

1. **Extra time investment:** Each press release site has its own interface, its own unique requirements, its own nuances, upgrades, etc. and unlike the major press release sites, you'll need to plan ahead. Many free press release sites have limited editorial desk/customer service hours, often requiring you submit your online press release 48 hours in advance. Is the extra time you're spending on increased labor worth what you're saving by going the free route?

2. **Minimal online exposure and visibility:** You can't rely on a single free press release site to deliver the typical coverage and exposure you receive from a paid site. Granted, you can increase visibility by paying to upgrade (see #3) but then that's not a free press release

site and it is costing you, right? There is also a time component, since you'll need to submit to multiple free sites to get the exposure you'd receive from one of the paid sites.

3. **Upgrades like links and pictures cost extra:** Free sometimes costs money, especially for features and functionality that are already bundled in with paid newswires. Again, compare and contrast. Ordering numerous upgrades ala carte may end up costing more than a paid newswire that includes several at one fixed price.

4. **Staying Power:** If you use a free press release site and you don't pay for archiving, then you have ZERO evergreen, seo and staying power.

5. **Performance metrics:** With free press release sites, performance metrics range from sketchy to non-existent. Many free and even paid providers offer more robust metrics for-you guessed it – an upgrade. There's an old saying "you can't improve what you can't measure."
Because of the limited nature of free press release metrics, you gain less

market knowledge and insights that you can funnel into future releases, thus improving performance over the long term.

A Sampling of Good Free Press/Media Release Distribution Websites

- www.prlog.org
- www.24-7pressrelease.com
- www.1888pressrelease.com
- www.clickpress.com
- express-press-release.net
- www.i-newswire.com
- www.pr.com
- www.pr9.net
- www.prcompass.com
- www.prurgent.com
- www.newsvine.com
- www.pitchengine.com
- www.openpr.com
- www.newswiretoday.com
- www.free-press-release.com
- www.sbwire.com
- www.myprgenie.com
- www.beforeitsnews.com
- www.onlineprnews.com
- www.bignews.biz
- www.BriefingWire.com

The Top Paid Press/Media Release Distribution Websites

Paid press release submissions sites will give you the deepest online coverage. Besides being in the news of the major search engines, your website will also get quality inbound links. Depending on the package you choose, some also offer additional features such as more anchor texts in your press release, analytics and even the option to embed a video for increased viewership.

- Businesswire.com
- Prnewswire.com
- Marketwire.com
- PRweb.com
- Webwire.com
- 24-7pressreleases.com
- Ereleases.com
- PRLeap.com
- Pressreleasepros.com
- www.pressrelease365.com
- www.sbwire.com
- www.pressmethod.com
- www.massmediadistribution.com

Great Tools to Track Your Footprints on the Internet

Social Mention: Mentions of your Name on the Social Web

A great tool for searching the social web, Social Mention offers a quick glance at mentions of your name on the Web. Enter your name and switch between blogs, microblogs, bookmarks, comments, events, images, news or all of them at once. RSS is available.

Pipl: Searching the Invisible Web

Pipl claims to search the deep or invisible Web to find documents, blog entries, photos, publicly available information that other search engines don't serve up. It's a great, fast search engine but it offers no RSS feed.

Monitter: Tracking Twitter

Monitter is one of the coolest looking monitoring tools for Twitter and one of the most useful. Although most people are using

Twitter's own search tool for search and alerts on Twitter, Monitter offers a little bit more. Giving you the option to search for three different keywords at once, Monitter is great if you want to keep your eye out for mentions of your name, your username and your company all at the same time. It offers an RSS feed. Monitter also allows you to narrow the search to a particular geographic location, allowing you to find focus on local news.

BoardTracker: The Ultimate Search Tool for Forums

BoardTracker is a forum search engine, message tracking and instant alert system offering relevant results quickly. It's a great search tool for forums and message boards.

Google Alerts: The Big G

Although Microsoft and Yahoo have alert tools, I find that Google's offering beats them hands down. It offers e-mail and RSS alerts for any set of keywords including your name.

Acknowledgments

I want to offer my deepest gratitude to Bonnie Rubin, George Stephanopoulos, Robin Roberts, Susan Donaldson James, Jerry Davich and Tonisha Pinckney for being so respectful to our family, our story and our mission. Your sensitivity and interest in increasing the awareness of FASD continues to help us in our mission to prevent it. While too numerous to list, I am humbly grateful for every one of you who supported our family through the bumps and bruises along the way to starting a national discussion. You know who you are and your presence in our lives is a blessing.

About The Author

Lori Gertz was raised on a dead end street on an island in the middle of the Connecticut River. She graduated from the University of Massachusetts, Amherst with honors in Journalism. Lori packed her drive, ambition and a few clothes into an overnight bag and didn't even wait for the ink on the diploma to dry before moving to NYC to pursue her career aspirations in the publishing business.

After 14 years in magazine publishing, Lori left NYC for places with bigger skies and a more manageable pace. Her dream to start a shoot-from-the-hip strategic marketing agency was realized when she founded Freakin' Genius Marketing based in a Chicago suburb, and now with offices in sunny Southern California.

She met her husband Craig on a carefully choreographed blind date in Chicago and became mother to their three children in the six years that followed. Lori loves to write and tell stories. She's penned dozens of articles and longstanding blogs, including a marketing blog (www.freakingeniusmarketing.blogspot.com), and a personal blog documenting her parenting experiences. Be The News is her first book. She is busily working on her second.

When she's not deep into a marketing gig or consulting with others to take their news national, renovating an old home, studying alternative medicine and Homeopathy, reading, or writing to excess and express, she facilitates on-site marketing workshops and seminars. In 2011, she and her husband relocated to California with two of their children and their three dogs. Their daughter Emily continues to live with her guardians.

For a personal consultation email Lori at
freakingeniusmarketing@gmail.com.
Find her on Twitter @lorigertzauthor,
Find her on Facebook at **www.facebook.com/bethenews,**
& on the web at
www.freakingeniusmarketing.com &
www.lorigertz.com

Coming Soon from author Lori Gertz

When Mama Can't Kiss It Better

Early Reviews

"This is an important book that psychologists have been waiting for. WHEN MAMA CAN'T KISS IT BETTER reminds us that some children are so severely damaged that even excellent parents cannot reverse the genetic imprint." --*Roberta Temes, Ph.D., Clinical Assistant Professor, Downstate Medical School Psychotherapist*

"Lori Gertz's heart-rending story speaks to every mother who has ever doubted herself and desperately longed for certainty when making crucial decisions about her children's welfare based on patchy information. WHEN MAMA CAN'T KISS IT BETTER is a harrowing portrait of what special needs parents go through when trying to find answers and resources. It exposes the frustrations and pitfalls of dealing with medical, legal, and educational systems that are inadequate to meet the needs of a rapidly growing population of children with serious developmental, emotional, and behavioral issues."--*Nancy Peske, coauthor of the award-winning Raising a Sensory Smart Child: The Definitive Handbook for Helping Your Child with Sensory Processing Issues*

Excerpt from *When Mama Can't Kiss It Better*

I didn't want to call the police today. I just wanted to go sledding.

Desperate to get away from the madness that felt like it was absorbing into my skin, I grabbed the pile of gloves, hats, and sweaters I had rummaged through before the episode began. Then I watched myself turn the knob on the door to my escape.

I needed a shower. I had been bitten, spat upon, and shouted at. I felt filthy and hopeless and useless and angry and desperately sad, but I had to perk myself up so I would appear excited and cheerful when the other children saw me.

I gently slid my way across the slippery sidewalk to the car. Craig's footprints of his struggle with Emily were but a faint abstract on the canvas of snow and concrete.

The kids were delighted to see me but disappointed that Emily and Daddy would not be joining us. I took a deep breath, cleaned my hands with antibacterial gel I keep in the side pocket of my door, and put the car in reverse.

Not a minute later, I looked in my rearview mirror to see Craig, halfway down our snow-covered street, running after Emily. She tore down the street as he raced after her, neither of them in coats, no socks or shoes on her feet. Frosty smoke came from her mouth as she screamed. I slowed down, and she ran past us towards the thoroughfare in search of harm. Self-harm. She was intent on finding a truck with the engraving to her headstone on it. She wanted to die. Craig chased after her. *Please dear God, my family needs you. Please see us in your crystal ball or however you keep track of all of us and help my little girl.*

Discreetly, I took a deep breath and tried to keep the pieces of my heart glued together.

"Mommy, there's Emily," Olivia squealed as I kept driving.

"Mommy, Daddy is chasing after her. She's in her bare feet, Mommy!"

"Mom, what if Dad doesn't catch her? She's trying to run into traffic again," Gabriel anxiously posed from the back seat.

"Guys, Daddy has Emily covered." I tried to assure them as much as I tried to assure myself. *Daddy has Emily covered.*

The adrenaline was rushing through my veins but I was intent not to let it overwhelm me. I inhaled a deep breath and held it for a few seconds to find my grounding. *I'm here, I'm safe, everything is okay now.*

"When I was a kid, we had a huge hill in our backyard," I chimed, perhaps a little too loudly and a little too purposely.

Amazed at how easily I could redirect their attention, I kept storytelling.

"The moment the snow would start, I'd be out there sledding. Of course, at the bottom of the hill there was a barn."

I could see them look at one another.

"I'd slam right into the side of the barn, pull myself together and yank the sled to the top and do it over and over and over again."

"Ahhh," Gabriel said, "that explains so much!"

He laughed. She laughed. I laughed.

I was talking and the words were coming out and they were listening and laughing, but it was as if I were having an out-of-body experience. I was still being assaulted on the floor between the kitchen and the pantry, just outside the laundry room, and my dream for one of my children was dying in my rearview mirror.

**

"Youramonsterfuck!"

In what kind of world do these words not even register on a mommy meter? Mine. A week prior I was wrenching my hands and tight-lipped as I nodded to directions I was being given in my seven year old's hospital discharge meeting.

"Emily's self-abuse is a pattern. She is unable to modulate herself. Your call to action is to use restraint until you can no longer handle it, try to move her to a safe space, and call the police," instructed her psychiatrist, one of four in the meeting after her most recent psych ward stay. The professionals rarely left room for me to love her with all the instructions she now came with.

My mind wandered to happy times. Happy Feet times. The scent of an old room still reminds me of the ancient auditorium where my beautiful little princess, dressed as a penguin, performed the exact dance she had been painfully practicing for a year.

Ten months of that year were a blur of deterioration during which she would melt onto the dance floor crying that she couldn't keep up or remember the dance. The final two months turned around by a short-lived success from an unusual alternative therapy.

I jumped from my seat and thwacked my hands together so hard and so many times I should have been flying. There she stood, on that stage surrounded by ten other little girls in penguin outfits. Orange and black. She was glowing. The lyrics of *Hit Me Up* filled the room as I watched her move to a perfectly choreographed dance performance. Tears streamed down my cheeks like a chocolate fountain as my pride raised me to a state of true joy. I couldn't feel the floor under my feet. *Baby! Baby! Just a little bit. Baby! Baby! Just a little more.*

"Shap-pow?" she had asked as I worked diligently before the performance to affix the small orange headpiece to her tiny little head, bobby pins hanging out from my lips like some crazy walrus.

"Chapeaux," I repeated still pinching my lips to hold the remaining pins. "It's French for hat. I didn't know that penguins wore them," I said smiling as I tipped hers to one side and stepped back to get a whole eyeful of my adorable penguin.

She was deliriously excited. I worried it would overwhelm her once on stage, but she was the star of the show and it filled up my bucket with love and pride and hope. I turned to Craig, who was also on his feet, fingers in his mouth whistling like a teapot.

Say hey, Come hit me up. Come hit me up. Baby! Baby! Just a little bit. Baby! Baby! Just a little more...rock to me, talk to me, handle me right ...

Like an invisible force, the words "I HATE YOU!" pushed me back into my skin. My happy princess penguin now just a memory as I found myself watching the nightmare ensuing on the kitchen floor as though it was happening to someone else.

"Youramonsterfuck!" The force of the words were so hard this time that spit flew out of her mouth onto my cheek.

I glanced over my shoulder. Craig looked dejected. He had gone almost completely gray in the last year, and he looked tired and pissed even when he rolled over after a decent night's sleep. This wasn't the man I married 12 years prior, any more than I was the woman he chose to be his wife.

I crouched over her, trying with all my might to restrain her thrashing arms and legs. Her eyes were daggers shooting up at me. Seething with rage, she kept screaming nonsensical obscenities and threats in my face. Her pink hooded snow jacket twisted upwards as she wriggled and I could see her tiny bellybutton and soft, childlike skin. I was floored by how small yet powerful she was. A size 5T dress with a Grand Canyon sized anger.

I kept trying to rationalize and reason with her.

"Emily, calm down," I begged. *Jesus!* I thought. We just wanted to do something as a family, but before I realized it, I was pouring my heart out to a furious beast who had no way of taking in what I was saying.

"Please, Emily. *Where are you? Where is my little girl?* I miss my family. I miss being able to go anywhere and do anything with all of us. I miss my husband, my best friend. I miss *you* baby girl. Please. Calm down. Please." My "reveal" now out there for all to see, she just kept raging. The words—"fuck" "monster" "liar" "hate you all"—washed over me like water dripping down the outside of a glass window during a heavy rainstorm.

As I watched 9 minutes on the oven clock tick by, she didn't seem to be tiring, but I was. It occurred to me that my two other children, ten-year-old Gabriel and four-year-old Olivia, were still waiting in the car in the driveway, though it was running and heated. They were used to Emily throwing a wrench in the day's events, used to going everywhere as a splintered family—two cars, one parent, always separated. This tantrum was probably just a small blip on their radar screen.

I was sweating now, dripping in fact, and hunched over Emily. She was sweating, too. Her face was bright red, her eyes fierce, as if she were a cornered animal ready to attack. I looked back at Craig again. I didn't have much left in me and her fury was not subsiding.

With whatever strength I had, I jumped back off her like a stealth cat, and somehow avoided the leg and arm that escaped my restraint and hit me hard in the rib as she flailed wildly.

She immediately sat up and began to slam her head on the side of the oven and then on the floor.

While she busied herself with biting her arm, alternating between the oven slams and hitting herself in the head with her own hands, she ripped off her outer clothes. I turned to Craig to decide what we would do. The situation was hopeless.

Forget the sledding, this was our life. This was a microcosm of every single day behind our proverbial white picket fence—this is what it was like here, right here, with our dual incomes, our rarified zip code, our over-mortgaged cedar home in the woods, our three kids and four dogs, and our dissolving family and marriage.

Craig and I barked quick suggestions at one another. I was dressed for sledding though I had nearly sweat through a waterproof coat. He had managed to slip out of his coat and boots after carrying her twisting, squirming body through the laundry room door at the start of this mess.

"You go," he said, almost yelling as he pointed toward the door. The window was covered with wet, gloppy snowflakes that were sliding down like sad faces. "I stay!"

He hadn't been coping well with her as of late. I pictured him trying to wrangle her in his arms while she kicked and bit him as he attempted to carry her up the stairs to her safe place in the tent in her room. Would he be able to handle her savage breakdown after I left?

"Just go. I have this," he said.

Our prolific conversations long gone, communication with one another had been reduced in recent years to pronouns and verbs. YOU GO! I STAY! GET HER! RUN! RUN FASTER! GOT HER! CALL DOCTOR! HOSPITAL NOW! Now CALL POLICE had been added to the list, but I didn't want to call them, all I wanted to do was go sledding.

###